Make Money Online To Achieve Freedom

LELA GIBSON

LELA GIBSON

CONTENTS

Freedom

How To Make Money Online And Become Financially Free By Creating Passive Income

Lela Gibson

Introduction

I want to thank you and congratulate you for buying the book, *"Freedom: How to Make Money Online and Become Financially Free by Creating Passive Income"*.

This book has lots of actionable information that you can use to make money online and become financially free by creating passive income.

Do you know the sweetest thing in the world? Well, one word; freedom! More precisely, the *freedom from the confines of a 9-5 job!* Unfortunately, freedom is not easy to come by since we live in a currency driven world where financial freedom is a fickle mistress. Even so, the best way to create financial freedom is by starting a business that earns you a passive income.

With the advancement of technology, anyone can invest online and start generating, hundreds, thousands and even millions of dollars. However, the success of your online business depends on some things such as your business idea and your business managerial prowess.

If you are ready to start an online business but are unsure of where to start or how to go about it, do not worry; this passive income guide will equip you with valuable knowledge guaranteed to help you start an online business that earns you a passive income.

Thanks again for buying this book. I hope you enjoy it!

Before you can learn the specifics of building a passive income, it is critical that you understand what you are venturing into so that you don't start with a wrong idea of what it is you are working towards as well as what to expect from your efforts. Let's begin.

Passive Income: A Comprehensive Background

A passive income, also called a residual income, is simply the money you earn when you are not actively working. If you are actively working, it means you will receive some money (active income), which, when you stop working, you stop earning. With contract work or active work, you have to do some work to receive pay. In other words, you MUST exchange your time (hours, minutes, days, weeks or even months) for pay. In that case, if you are not working, you cannot be paid; it is simple logic!

This is always not the case with a passive income. With passive incomes, you earn whether you work actively or not. To create a passive income stream, you will have to put in some work upfront to get the ball rolling. You will however get to a point where your income stream will become passive such that it generates revenue on its own without you having to work for it. Think of publishing a book on Amazon for instance.

After doing the upfront work of writing and promoting the book in its initial stages, you will get to a point whereby the book can continue making money whether you do anything to promote it or not. That's passive income!

Before we head any further, we have to discuss some things about a passive income because these things are important and will help you understand the nature of a passive income. Some of these include:

1: *Passive incomes are often not permanent incomes:* Get it right: some online passive incomes may last for years, decades, or even centuries. They can however never be permanent. This is because all forms of income eventually dry up at a given point for one reason or another.

2: *It is not a one-time lump sum payment:* Some incomes such as inheritance, sale of assets like pieces of land, or sale of stocks are one-time lump sum payments. This is not the case with passive income since a passive income is a source of income that has a sense of continuity over a certain period.

3: *Some passive incomes are semi-passive:* You may be your own boss but you will need to do some work (even if its management), although you will not receive pay for maintaining your investment.

For instance, if you build a house and rent it out, you will definitely receive your passive income from the tenants but when they move out, you will have to invest some energy, money, and time to maintain the vacated premise and seek other tenants.

4: *Passive income streams need maintenance:* Whether it is checking emails or paying taxes on your passive income, you have to do some of these activities for maintenance since they keep your source of passive income going.

5: *Your passive income might be another person's active Income:* No matter what kind of online business you invest in, you will have to hire people to do some work that help you earn your passive income. In other words, your passive income builds on leveraging on other people's active income to succeed! For example, if you have a freelance writing marketplace for instance, you will have to hire some people who will be writing or editing your articles. You will have to pay them hence they will receive active income but their work is what shall help you earn a passive income.

Now that we have established these critical things about passive income streams, the next thing we have to consider is why the internet is the best way to create multiple passive income streams.

Why the Internet—The Internet as a Way to Earn Passive Income

Online investments are a true deal. If you are doubtful of this, just look at Mark Zuckerberg, the creator of the Facebook. Can you guess his worth? He is worth about $53.5 billion and his worth is rapidly increasing on a day-by-day basis. Do you know what perhaps makes Facebook, which has been in business for slightly over 13 years (founded in 2004) such a huge success? Well, because it is deployed on a massive scale through the internet; all that the employees at Facebook need to do is to keep the system functional (system in this case is website, servers, new functionalities etc.) and the rest is income being made on autopilot; no one goes to a Facebook offline shop to make a payment- everything is done automatically! Well, you don't have to create the next Facebook; the point I am making here is that once deployed, the earning potential is literally limitless!

Another online source of passive income is music. Look at Justin Bieber, a teen pop singer whose career started through YouTube; over the last 2 years, Bieber has earned more than $108 million.

Karmin is another pop duo who signed a million dollar deal with Chris Brown after their cover of the original "Look at Me Now" went viral and generated more than 100 million views.

When it comes to blogs and websites, look at John Wu, the founder of Bankaholic.com website. In 2008, he managed to sell his website for $14.9 million. That's not all; in 2010, Michael Arrington sold his Entrepreneurial tech blog site *TechCrunch* to AOL for a staggering $30 million.

We cannot forget to mention fashion bloggers such as Leandra Medine. Medinefounded the Man Repeller blog. Her website grew so popular that it gave birth to two jewelry lines (collaboration with Dannijo and Del Toro), earning her $325, 000.

Sophia Amoruso, the founder of Nasty Gal online clothing store started by selling vintage items on eBay, a project that built her fan-base and upon outgrowing her platform, she started her own clothing store. Today, the Nasty Gal clothing store is worth $130 million.

Authors earn a passive income too. For example, Louise Ross, the author of the romance thriller 'Holy Island' sold more than 100, 000 copies (online) in less than a year. This book earned her about $1 million despite even after rejection from a number of publishers.

Yes, it has happened and it is still happening: thousands of people are using the internet to create passive income streams. What are you waiting for? Your talent or passion might make you the next internet millionaire or even billionaire if you put your mind to it. As they say, it is better to try and fail (which of course you will not because you have this book to guide you and give you the secret to internet business success) than to never try at all.

You may be one of the lucky few who shoot funny or crazy videos and post them on YouTube and within no time, the video has more likes and views than you can imagine. This video might prompt YouTube to get in touch with you asking for partnership. Do you know what that means? YouTube will run ads on your popular channel and share the revenue with you! How cool is that? Well, besides that, you stand to derive many other benefits from building a passive income online.

Why You MUST Build An Online Passive Income Stream

Some of the benefits you can get from an online passive income include the following:

You Become Your Own Boss

By having an online business or investment that generates a passive income, you automatically become your own boss. This means you can do whatever you want and plan for your hours without any limitations. This is very dissimilar to an active income stream where your boss will plan for your hours.

When you start a profitable online business, you will be making your own schedule. Imagine working for 3-4 hours and then spending the rest of your time doing other things such as pursuing your hobbies or spending time with your friends or family. This is a very interesting idea, one most people do not get to do.

Lower Taxes

When you start your passive income stream, you will pay fewer taxes because business taxes are lower for online businesses than taxes for active jobs hence, only a small amount of your passive income will go to taxes.

Unlimited Income Potential

With active work, no matter how much work you do or how many raises you get, there will always be a ceiling. Your boss will always pay you the agreed amount. And you can only work for so many hours. Even if you climb up the corporate ladder fast, you can bet that if you are exchanging your time for money, your earning potential is limited.

But with passive income businesses (if set properly), your earning potential is limitless. With all online sources of passive income, you will not have any limitation to the amount you earn. The amount you earn will depend on how well you establish your source of income following the right steps (we shall see these later).

Creativity Freedom

It is your job; you responsible for setting the goals, missions, and visions of your investment. This will allow you the opportunity to think and consult different people for different ideas. Above all, you will always make the final decisions. You will have the freedom to be creative, an opportunity that will motivate you to work towards your set goals. This is unlike most active work where you have to follow a certain method set by your boss or the company you work for.

Location Independence

For most active income streams, you will have a fixed workplace where you will have to report on time every day as agreed. Your fixed work area could be a cubicle your boss gave you as your workstation probably because he wants to track you as you work.

For online passive incomes, no one is there to watch you or track your movements during work hours because you are your own boss and you can do whatever you want. The most important thing in online passive work is a computer, and an access to the internet.

You can carry your personal computer to the beach, to your home, or even in your vehicle, coffee shop, and still work from there. It is up to you to decide whether to have a fixed workplace or not.

Even with its lucrative outlook, passive income has many misconceptions some of which we will debunk next.

Passive Income Misconceptions

Because it is gaining rapid popularity, online passive income streams are generating tons of myths and misconceptions. Let us bust some of the main ones:

You Just Need a Couple of Days to Make Thousands of Dollars Passively Online

If you thought that you would just create an idea such as a video, post it on YouTube, and then after a few days, you wake up with thousands of dollars in your bank account, you are so wrong. It will take months or even years to create a good business out of your idea.

For example, if you want to create something you think your community wants, the first thing you have to do is to lay the groundwork, research what they need, and then figure out how best to give it to them (an activity that could take months or years).

Passive Income is 100% Passive

Whether your project requires maintenance or not, you will have to work even if the only work you do is setting up things at the beginning of your project. No income is 100% passive; if you thought you do not need to work to start or maintain your passive income stream, think again.

Even after your business has a stable base and is earning you great amounts of money, you will still have do work adjacent things such as checking your pages or links in case of breakdowns or update a website theme. For sustainability, you also must know what your customers think about your product, carry out tests to know what works and what doesn't etc.

You also need to keep in mind that things change. You have to be on the lookout for new information that may be relevant to your product. This means that at some point, you may have to update your product so that it continues to remain relevant to your customers.

Having Employees Will Make Your Work Harder

You might want to work alone because you think you will succeed easily. However, the truth is that utilizing teams for your online passive business has many benefits such as:

1. You can be a source of income to other people hence contributing to their success.

2. Your employees can run your business for you hence allowing you time to do other things. As a rule, you should learn to delegate things that others can do for you. For example, if you have a blog, you can get someone to run your social media accounts so that you can concentrate on creating content.

3. By having a team, you will be opening yourself and your business up for more opportunities because they will help you sell your idea. However, you must be willing to listen to your team. If they know you value their opinion, they will be more likely to run their ideas by you.

If you want great employees, take a few minutes of your time to train them. Let them know exactly what you expect of them instead of giving them vague instructions. This way, you will all be on the same page as far as your business is concerned. You'll also be able to rest easy knowing that you're all working towards the same goal.

It Is Easy Money

Many people think generating an online passive income is an easy way to earn money but the truth is; while this may be so, it is not always the case. Every business or investment will need some capital, time, and energy.

You will come across many competitors because you are not the only player in the game. As a result, you will have to work hard to keep up with the competition. You will have to do something more to stay one-step ahead. If you thought you would sleep all day and then find money in your bank account in the evening, it is best to wake up now and start figuring out what you want to do.

Now that we have looked at the benefits of running an online passive income business as well as busted some of the myths surrounding passive income, the next question is; which types of online businesses can you run online to generate passive income for you? That's what we will discuss next.

Online Passive Income Streams

There are many online business ideas you can start today and start earning a passive income. Some of these include:

Make Passive Income Through Blogging

Blogging is increasingly becoming very popular these days thanks to the endless ways it makes the bloggers to derive satisfaction from their readers (through income, engagement etc.). And given that a blog can give you an endless list of ways through which you can make money once you have build a readership (I will show you how), this makes blogs a core part of every successful online business. So how can you go about creating a successful blog? That's what we will discuss next.

How to Start Blogging for Money

To create a revenue generating blog, do the following:

Step 1: Start a Blog

If you want to use blogging to create a passive income stream, you must have a blog. If you do not have one, no worries; here are the steps you should follow to create your blog.

Decide On What to Blog About

The main aim of any blog is to become the recommended resource for its topic of discussion. Before you decide on what to blog about, make sure to choose a topic that you enjoy, a topic with plenty of room for discussion, and most importantly, a topic you can easily establish yourself as an authority. You can learn how to choose something to blog about here.

Choose a Platform

The internet has many services that can help you start a blog (platforms) that may leave you confused without knowing what to go for. Do not go for a free service; you might want to save a dollar or two but remember that investing in a good platform is a determinant of how much you will earn from your blog. WordPress is an inexpensive, flexible, easy to use, and popular platform you can try. You can learn how to choose a blogging platform here.

Choose a Domain Name (Web Address)

If you do not have a domain name, you have to come up with one. It might not be hard to come up with a name but coming up with a good, unique name no one owns may be a tad difficult. If you find it hard to come up with your own name, you can visit a platform such as namemesh to generate domain name ideas and then use a domain name registrar such as GoDaddy.com, iPage.com, Hostgator.com, Bluehost.com or NameCheap.com to register your domain. You can learn more on how to choose a domain name here.

Choose a Web Host

Finding a good web host will allow other people to find your site on the internet. Many of the free or cheap web hosts available today will tempt you to sign up. However, to be a successful blogger, it is critical that you opt for a self hosted blog, which is where the need to choose a web host comes in. The thing is; many of the companies that sell domain names also offer web hosting services. Therefore, feel free to try their service. You can check some of the points to consider when choosing a web host here.

After you have selected a niche, chosen a domain name and have your blog hosted, you can move on to the next step, which is to set up your blog. Assuming that you are using WordPress.org, you need to install it on your web host; there is usually a one click install button when you have logged in to your control panel; use that to install WordPress. After that, you will need to actually set up the blog to be the way you want it to look like. You can learn how to go about it here and here or simply search "How to set up a WordPress blog" on YouTube- video tutorials are best!

As you set up your blog, it is also important to make your blog search engine friendly. You can do that by optimizing your blog for search engines to ensure you generate organic traffic (this is the traffic that comes to your website after someone keys in certain keywords on their preferred search engine).

You can learn how to set up your blog for search engines here, here, here and here.

Step 2: Create Content

For your blog to generate a passive income, you have to create useful content on your chosen topic to attract readers. Most readers like blogs that talk about:

Solving problems: We hate feeling frustrated. If you can think of something that frustrates many people and you can post a good solution to it, start writing the solution, and see how you can have many readers.

Reaching a goal: Do you have a goal you once set, reached it (for example getting out of debt or losing weight), and you think many people have the same goal but do not know how to go about achieving it? This is a prime chance to earn a passive income. Simply spell out what you did and how you did it to inspire others in similar situations.

Entertainment: If you lead a wildly interesting life or are outrageously funny, you can create entertainment blogs. The only thing you need is creativity that will help you create a uniquely entertaining story. You can also make your story entertaining and at the same time helpful.

For example, if you keep camels at home and you decide to write an interesting story about camels, do not just mention that you raise them; you can include some information on how you do it. From this, you are likely to attract many readers because your story will be entertaining and helpful.

The thing about content is that readers want quality content that meets their expectations. You MUST strive to fulfill that expectation by publishing high quality blog posts frequently.

As you publish great content, don't forget to start building a readership for your blog.

Step 3: Build a Social Media Relationship

You may be creating great content but getting very few readers because of a bad social media presence. Be active: participate on social media group discussions, comment on other people's blogs, and find people who could benefit from your blog and be friendly to them. If they find your blog interesting, these people will help you by recommending your blog posts to their social circles.

Always remember to use social media sites where most of your target audience hangs out. For example, if you write an entertainment blog, Facebook, Twitter and Instagram are probably the best sites for you.

Note: As a rule of thumb, make sure every blog post is optimized for sharing on the different platforms and have social sharing buttons at the bottom of every post. You can set up every post for sharing on social platforms by making sure each post has great images, infographic, GIF and other types of images to increase their ease of sharing; people love visually appealing content!

Step 4: Build a Strong Platform

You have to continue researching so that you can improve your craft knowledge and increase your valuable and deep content output and thus create a super strong platform. In addition, it is also important to consider the type of reputation you want to have. How do you want your readers to perceive you? What do you want them to know you for? Brand your name and your work.

Here are some of the things that will help you build a strong platform:

Have a good headshot and consistent avatar: That small photo you attached to your social media sites is very important. Look for a good photographer or take good photo. Attach it where you should attach it and leave it there as your logo. This image will associate with all your work.

Do not change your avatar any time you want because doing so will confuse your readers: Imagine how confusing it would be if a famous company kept changing its logo every week. This is what you do to your readers if you whimsically change your avatar! Choose one avatar you will use across the internet to ensure consistency.

Post carefully and thoughtfully: You definitely have competitors who want to see you fail. To avoid their victory, write and share carefully if you do not want things and stuffs that are private or anonymous coming back to haunt you in the future. You can share something with a friend and within no time, it goes viral, ruining your reputation. So yeah, be careful with what you post online.

You should also be careful when it comes to replying to accusations and criticism. Yes, you may want to lash out at someone who is abusive towards you. But if you do so, you'll only alienate others. On the other hand, if you respectfully state your position and acknowledge any failure, you will have the opportunity to mend relationships and create an environment where critical discussions are welcome. This will keep your customers coming back.

Be aware: Not only should you be careful about what you post but you should also be aware of its implications. Let's put it this way. Many 'innocent statements' can land you in trouble because of your wording. This is especially so when you use social media platforms that require you to post in brief. Before you put that post button, make sure that your words do not alienate any group unless that is your intention.

Be real: Some bloggers portray themselves one way online when they are something different in real life. This is a very wrong way of building a platform because one day, your online and offline worlds will collide and you will lose many readers because they will realize you have been dishonest.

To avoid this, make your two worlds congruent. If you have decided to portray a particular quality online, try as much as possible to make it your real life quality. While we're on the subject, you need to determine how much of your personal life you're willing to expose to the world. Determine what to share and what to keep private. There is such a thing as 'too much information'.

Step 5: Choose Your Monetization Options

The number of ways through which you can monetize your blog is literally limitless especially because almost all the other methods of making money online can to be backed/supported by a blog or website if they are to succeed.

Here are some ways through which you can monetize your blogs:

Displaying ads: I want you to think of your blog as a TV station and your audience as the viewers; the bigger your audience is, the more the earning potential for advertising. There are different forms of advertising though; direct advertising and using ad networks. With direct advertising, you agree with an individual or company to display ads about their product/service for a given period for a fee. With ad networks however, you register to an ad network then connect your blog to the network so that the network can display relevant ads on your blog to your audience. In this case, if you go for an ad network, you are paid for every click. Some popular ad networks include:

- Google AdSense

- RevContent

- Adsterra

- Ad Maven

- AdRecover

- BlogAds

- Media.Net

- Advertising.com

- Clicksor

- Chitika

- AdCash

- PropellerAds

- InfoLinks

- Adbuff

- AdBlade

- BidVertiser

When starting out, ad networks are the best option for you because they don't have requirements that are too high and the fact that they look for the paying advertisers (customers) so that you can focus on creating great content that keeps your visitors coming back to your blog. The only downside to this method is that you really need a lot of visitors to make any significant amount of money from blogging.

As your blog grows and depending on its nature, you can then start doing **sponsored posts** i.e. you publish a blog about a certain brand, service or issue of interest to another person for a small fee.

Besides advertising, you can use your blog to make money in other ways including:

- Affiliate marketing

- Selling your own products/services

- Supporting your publishing business

- Having a membership site

- Selling courses

- And much, much more!

We will discuss some of these ways as we go on starting with affiliate marketing.

Make Passive Income Through Affiliation Marketing

This is a passive income stream where your blog acts like a salesperson for selling other people's products online. When someone buys a product through your referral link, you earn a commission. Some products pay as high as 80-90% commissions, especially digital downloadable products. Physical products and services (where active work is involved) typically pay less affiliate commissions (5-20% maybe).

The thing with blogging and earning affiliate income is that when you develop a loyal audience, you can bet that they are likely to want to buy whatever products/services you are recommending, which essentially means your earning potential is high. All you have to do is to post a blog post with a link to the affiliate product, share it on social media and to your mailing list then wait for your affiliate commissions to start streaming in. The larger your loyal audience, the greater your earning potential.

The good thing about affiliate marketing is that there are no investments, no inventory, no product shipping, no fees, and above all, your blog will be around for many years meaning you will end up earning money from a link you posted immediately after your now 5-year old blog.

How to get started With Affiliate Marketing

To get started with affiliate marketing:

If you already have a blog (we learnt how to go about it in the previous chapter), you don't need to create any other website; you can start right away.

Join Affiliate Programs

You can join many of the available affiliate programs; examples include:

- Avangate
- CJ
- ClickBank
- Rakuten Affiliate Network
- ShareASale
- Amazon Associates
- JVZoo
- eBay Partner Network
- MaxBounty
- Flex Offers
- AvantLink

All you have to do is to join any of the above programs, see how they work and perhaps start promoting products that are relevant to whatever it is you are blogging about, as this makes it easy to promote/recommend products to your current audience. Upon registration, you will receive an affiliate ID and perhaps a unique link for every product that you are promoting to help the company and yourself to track affiliate sales, as well as commissions. Simply figure out how a certain product will make the lives of your audience better when posting a blog post/sending an email to your email subscribers (yes, your blog needs to have an email opt-in form to help you to collect your audience's email addresses so that you can reach out to them later).

Obviously, the above list does not in any way represent all the affiliate programs out there. You can simply search "affiliate networks" on your favorite search engine to display some more.

Some products/service may have affiliate programs not listed on the website. If you love a product and you cannot see its affiliate program on its website, contact the company to see if they have an affiliate program. For most companies, it is free to become an affiliate. If a company is asking you to pay a fee to join its affiliate program, you are staring at a scam. Therefore, always be careful.

So what are your options as far as posting content that helps you to generate leads and perhaps earn you a commission in the end? Let's discuss that next.

Step 3: Link Promotion

There are different ways to promote your affiliate links. They include:

Comparing products: You can decide to write content comparing 2 or several products. This will help your readers make purchase decision by weighing the pros and cons of each product. The thing is; whichever option that people choose, you can stand a chance to earn affiliate commissions in the process. You can compare the products side by side (in a table) or compare them in pros (where you discuss the pros and cons of each).

Creating tutorials: You can decide to document anything that involves a process on YouTube videos. You can also document something already documented if you think you can do it better. By doing so, you will help your readers save time and money (since they will not have to watch all over for tutorials before they settle for the one they are looking for) and as a result, you will end up having many readers. With this approach, you can place your affiliate link on the video description.

Always mention the product in your content: This is an easy way to promote your link because all you will have to do is mention the product and hyperlink it. For example, if you are writing an article on how to cook pancakes, you can provide a link to where you buy certain ingredients for instance.

Product reviews: If you decide to write an in depth product review, all you need to do is provide your honest review of the product. If you write a glowing review for a bad product thinking you will earn an affiliate income, you are in for a rude shock. When your product reviews are honest, your readers will reward you (for loyalty) and above all, they will become lifetime fans who will read your blog posts and share them.

Look for coupon codes: People love freebies; your audience is not exempted! If you can get discount/coupon codes to some websites that allow affiliates, you can bet that you will have many people streaming to buy the product before the discount period runs out. Simply look for a product that your audience would love to have, have your affiliate link and then get a coupon code that they can key in at checkout; they will thank you and you will earn some money in the process.

Make Passive Income With Membership Site

A membership site is simply what it is; a membership site. People pay to be allowed to access content that is only available for members. You can create a membership area within your WordPress site using a plugin such as MemberPress or S2member.

So what is it that you can limit access to? Well, you can have a course where you teach your members something that you know best, have value added products, offer bundles/packages to books and other content that would make sense to pay for access etc. You can even have webinars, podcasts, ebooks and other types of content within the members area. So how exactly can you get started with a membership site? Let's discuss that next.

How to Get Started With Membership Sites

To start your membership site:

Step 1: Create a Membership Site (With WordPress)

From the above discussion, you already know how to create a website using WordPress. You will need this knowledge to create a membership site. WordPress is the best platform since it takes care of all back end stuff required to run a membership site.

Using WordPress, go to plugins, search for S2member plugin, and install it. Make sure to fill all fields such the price for your services and products and the payment details (on PayPal button) to ensure the visitors get the information they need to know before they subscribe.

Your visitors will join or subscribe to your membership site and make payments through the PayPal button to get a username and password (from you) which will help them access the member's area that has your products or services.

Remember to set up your membership site. This means you will have to fill "general option" tab and fill out all the fields to ensure your membership site is functioning well.

Membership sites often have membership levels with level 1 being the lowest and level 4 the highest. You need to set this up by selecting the level you want to restrict to paying members only and which level to designate to each post.

Step 2: Building a Membership Base

It might be difficult to get people willing to pay a fee for your site every month, but with the help of the following tips, you will build a strong membership site.

Build trust: To gain trust, you can offer a free trial. People like trying things out before purchasing them. When you use this method, you will increase your sign up rate and since you offer good products and services, you will get more members compared to if you did not have a free trial.

You can also decide to offer a free level of membership. Leaving one level free and charging the rest will also get you more members and within no time, the amount of money your site generates in a month will surprise you. You can use Wishlist Member plugin to offer some freebies.

You can also build trust by building your membership base on a separate site using the same niche (your blog is good enough if you are serious about it). Building a free membership base and letting people use it will earn you trust and loyalty and every time you launch a new membership site using the same niche, you will have many subscribers.

Step 3: Drive Traffic to Your New Membership Site

You have to increase traffic to your blog by growing the list of loyal audience and raving fans. How can you do that? The first thing you need to do is to create a highly converting lead magnet. Some people call it bribes, content upgrades, freebies, or signup incentives.

A lead magnet is an irresistible 'bribe' where you can decide to offer a valuable service or content such as a 5 minutes free consultation, a free PDF checklist, a video, or eBook to your target audience in exchange for their contact information.

Whichever method or route you decide to use, make sure it is appealing to your target audience and it solves a common problem for your target audience. This will help you create a long-term audience relationship.

You can also drive traffic to your membership site by reaching out to influential bloggers. Instead of posting your content on social media and waiting for an influencer to notice it, directly pitch your content. If your content is valuable, influencers will share it with their social media followers. Do not just send your content to influential bloggers and wait for them to share it for you. Everybody it doing that, you need a better plan such as this one:

Choose your hit list: Identify about 20 influential bloggers who actively engage their/your target audience, accepts guest posts, and have some social authority.

Let them notice you: Subscribe or join their group. Read, comment, and share their blogs as many times as possible; this will ensure they notice you. It may take a couple of weeks to happen, but eventually, someone will take note. In addition, send them complimentary emails. It might sound like a lot of work, but the rewards are astonishing.

Send them a pitch email: Send them a quick, on point email asking them to check out your content. If your content is good, they will surely share it because you have already built a strong relationship with them.

Step 4: Keep Your Members Happy

If you want to keep your passive income flowing, keep its source (your members) happy. Do not give them a reason to unsubscribe from your site. To avoid this, provide your members with fresh, up to date, and valuable information.

Create different types of membership sites using software subscriber (the best license software where you pay a monthly or yearly fee to access your membership site). Some of the ideas you can post on your new membership sites are mentor blogs, offer services such as Forex tips, stocks, or sports betting tips, content addressing adults, or the community. Just remember to keep updating your membership site.

Step 5: Delegate Tasks

Having established different membership sites that generate a passive income, you can delegate some daily activities to get more time to think of new and good content you can use to create more and more sites.

Hire people to write your content (after you have drafted it) and let them respond to members' comments and requests. By doing so, you will have a chance to expand your income streams and drive them to a point where they can earn you thousands of dollars every day.

Passive Income Tips

As you go about creating passive income, some tips will come in handy. These include:

Prepare to teach, not to sell

When creating passive income, your focus should be on teaching, not on selling. You want to create a product that will be of value to your customers. If you concentrate on teaching, you will have an easier time creating passive income because all you have to do is write down the instructions step by step.

You should then get someone to test your product. This way, they can let you know if a certain step is missing. More often than not, what seems obvious to you will not be obvious to your customers. Thus, having a beta test will point out the flaws of your product and you can make changes before selling it to your customer.

Stop waiting for perfection

Yes, you want to sell the best product. However, you cannot wait around for perfection. The truth is you cannot place yourself in the shoes of all your potential customers. As much as you try, some things won't cross your mind. These are the things that you will learn only when your product is out. These things will become obvious through the feedback you get. Thus, set the production date and stick to it. Once you get feedback, determine which information is helpful to you and use it to upgrade your product.

Start building your list

Your list starts with one name and then it grows from there. Don't wait to become established before building your list. Why is list building important? Well, your list tells you that there are people interested in what you have to say. If your list is made up of an engaged audience, your chances of selling products goes up and that is good for you.

Yes, you can make passive income in several ways. However, at the end of the day, all you rely on are customers actually buying your product. Thus, create good products, build your customer base and create a great marketing strategy and you will succeed.

I need your help...

We have come to the end of the book. Thank you for reading and congratulations for reading until the end.

The above are not all the ways through which you can generate passive income online. You can try other methods like:

Selling your own products: If you can develop a software, plugin, theme, book, mobile app or any other digital product including photos, you can sell them online and make a passive income in the process. You can learn more about it here and here.

Peer-Peer lending: If you have some extra cash to spare, you can lend it to someone who is in need through various peer-peer lending platforms online. In the process, you earn a tidy interest (more than what you can earn from your bank). You can learn more about peer to peer lending here.

I believe all this information will help you to get started. Start your passive income project today. Do whatever it takes to develop and establish it, and wait for your reward (the great positive change in your financial status)

Finally, if you enjoyed this book, then I'd like to ask you for a favor, would you be kind enough to leave a review for this book on Amazon? It'd be greatly appreciated!

I want to reach as many people as I can with this book, and more reviews will help me accomplish that!

If you have any questions or problems, please contact us: hello@freedomdestination.com

Thank you and good luck!

Preview Of '20 Easy And Fast Diet Tips For Losing Weight'

Before we start learning about the strategies you can use to lose weight, let's start by highlighting some of the benefits that will come as a result of shedding those extra pounds just to give you extra motivation to want to do something NOW.

Why You Need To Lose Weight

Healthy weight loss has over one hundred benefits; these include emotional and physical benefits. I will dedicate this section to discussing the health benefits that many people (and weight loss/health books) do not pay enough attention to.

1: You Avoid Pre-Diabetes or Type 2 Diabetes

Pre-diabetes/high blood glucose is a condition that develops when the blood sugar levels in your blood move past normal ranges but not enough to qualify as diabetes. When your body stops consistently producing insulin sufficient to meet your body's needs, or the amount produced does not work properly, type 2 diabetes is likely to develop. Being pre-diabetic places you at a very high risk of developing type 2 diabetes.

Being obese or overweight is a proven leading risk factor for type 2 diabetes because carrying excess weight typically makes it hard for cells to respond to insulin, and since the additional fat acts as an insulating layer, it makes it more difficult for the sugar to enter the cells, which results in more circulating blood sugar levels.

Nonetheless, if you are already a pre-diabetic, you can prevent the progression to diabetes by shedding some weight (to reduce the insulating layer on cells so that they respond more to insulin) and trying to maintain a healthy weight.

2: You Keep Your Heart Healthy

When it comes to heart disease, some of the key risk factors are high cholesterol and high blood pressure. Research shows that:

1. Excessive accumulation of body fat makes your body release particular chemicals that occur naturally into the bloodstream, which increases blood pressure, and

2. Being overweight makes the liver produce too much amounts of Low density Lipoprotein (LDL) also called cholesterol. LDL tends to be sticky and gathers in the walls of blood vessels, which causes the narrowing of arteries, a condition called atherosclerosis, which increases your risk of strokes and heart attack.

When you lose weight, your blood pressure often reduces and the liver naturally reduces the amount of LDL it produces.

Royal Adelaide Hospital conducted a research on cardiovascular improvements with respect to a special weight loss program. Their results showed a decrease of cholesterol by 12%, a 10% decrease of LDL, a 5% decrease in diastolic blood pressure, and an 8% decrease in systolic blood pressure.

3: Improved Sleep (and Possible Treatment of Sleep Apnea)

One of the most prominent benefits of losing weight is improved sleep. When you gain excess weight, you gather more soft tissues in the neck; this intensifies the incidence of snoring.

NOTE: Snoring is a result of constricted airways, which obstructs air movement.

Snoring can be a symptom of sleep apnea, a possible life-threatening condition characterized by obstruction of breathing that requires the victim to wake up frequently from sleep to resume breathing.

As a victim of sleep apnea, you rarely remember anything about the episodes of waking many times a night to breathe but even so, this sleep and oxygen deprivation could easily lead to a weak immune system, high blood pressure, heart disease, memory problems, and sexual dysfunction.

When you lose weight, you reduce the amount of fatty tissue in the back of your throat, decrease snoring and the likelihood of the worsening of your health- as aforementioned. You encourage better sleep quality and reduce the risk of developing sleep apnea.

4: Better Joints (Mobile and Pain-Free)

Osteoarthritis (OA) is one of the most common joint disorders. It causes the tissues that protect the joints (cartilage and bone) to wear away. Consequently, the joints become tender and swollen, thus making movement very painful.

When you are overweight, you add to the load placed on the joints that bear the weight such as hips and knees.

NOTE: When you walk, you exert a force of approximately 3-6 times your entire body weight across the knee (read more on this page (check the discussion section) or here), so adding about 10 kg of weight does increase the force on the knees, which is equal to carrying 30-60 kgs^2 extra.

Therefore, a loss of merely 5% of your body weight could reduce the amount of stress placed on the knees, lower back, and hips, and reduce the pain (remember that losing 5kgs is equal to relieving a force of 15-30kgs^2 on the knees). According to doctors, a 10% loss of bodyweight has presented a 28% improvement in knee osteoarthritis symptoms.

Check out the rest of 20 Easy And Fast Diet Tips For Losing Weight on Amazon, go to:**http://amzn.to/2mNtPEg**

Online Business from Scratch

The 9 Step Guide to Building a Profitable and Sustainable Online Business

LELA GIBSON

INTRODUCTION

First and foremost, I want to thank you for buying this book. You have really taken the first step to becoming a successful online entrepreneur.

Why should you read this book until the end of it?

I have done my best to finally make a book that summarizes all the information that every online entrepreneur needs to know when they start an online business. I personally studied all these things for years. So I made the decision that I would write a book with all the information in one place.

This book has lots of actionable information that you can use to build your own online business from scratch or make your existing business more profitable. However, this is not "DFY" (done for you). It is a guide with all the most important strategies to create an online business that makes you passive income. You need to take action after you read this book.

Today the internet provides us with a lot of opportunities. Maybe you saw more people who can afford to work from home or even travel the world without having a 9-5 job. How can they do this? The answer is: with the internet. This is an opportunity, and I believe you should live with it.

Do you want a life where you're free to do whatever you want? Do you want a life without a 9-5 job with no boss? Well, the best way to live the life you want is to start a business that earns you a passive income. All you need is a laptop and internet access.

Okay, so how can this book help you with getting started?

First of all, I'll help you to evolve the right mindset and philosophy because there are so many cases where people fail to build a successful online business. Why? The first chapter will be about this.

Then you need to find your customers because you can't sell to everybody. Who are they? This is your niche.

If you'd like to make tons of money, not just some sales here and there, you need a brand. I will explain this in the third chapter.

That's great. However, you can have the most perfect product/service, the most perfect website, but if you don't have traffic, it's all useless. So then I'll give you some tips to get traffic. If you have traffic, you need to turn your visitors into customers and then repeat buyers. This requires the right strategy. You can find this strategy in the fifth chapter, How To Create An Online Business.

Every successful long-term business is about adding value and being helpful to their customers. Without that, your business will die. I believe this is the most important part of this book. This is a must in every business.

These are the core strategies, but I'll give you some practical tips too. In the seventh chapter, we'll discuss the marketing tips to get more customers and earn a lot more money. If you use these tips, you'll get a big traffic tsunami. The more traffic, the more customers, the more money you make.

In the eighth chapter, I'll write some examples of online money making opportunities. This will give you a big picture of online business models.

The ninth chapter is a more advanced lesson. This will be useful once you have gone through all the previous lessons and applied them to your online business. The same for the last chapter, which is a bonus section for people who want to learn more and committed enough to work really hard for their dreams. Okay, so let's get started. Move on to the first chapter and make sure to read the book until the end of it.

CONTENTS

Step 1: Why Do You Want To Build An Online Business And Why Do People Fail To Build One Successfully?

First, let me ask you a question. What does your dream life look like? Imagine that you're totally free. You don't have a 9-5 job, you don't have a boss. You can live wherever you want. You can do whatever you want. Imagine that. What would you do? You're able to travel the world, or you can spend all your time with your family. What is the most important thing to you? Please don't just read these questions, answer them too. Why do I ask these silly questions? Because building an online business requires hard work. So you need a 'why'. You need something that can motivate you when you have failures or just simply have a hard time. So first you need to know why you want to build an online business, what is your goal with it? It can be anything that can motivate you.

But why an online business? Today's world is all about technology and the internet. In fact, building an online business is easier, cheaper, and more profitable than building an offline business. You don't have to rent an office and pay a lot of money for offline advertising. You can start your own business with very little cost. However, you'll be able to make much more money than in an offline business in a much shorter period of time.

Last but not least, an online business can create a passive income so that you can live free. An online business can be automated. I think this is the most attractive reason. You might have to do some work with it, but you can work from wherever you want.

That's enough. I'm sure you already know what the advantages of building an online business are if you bought this book. So let's go over the next question, why do people fail to build a successful online business?

First, I want to clarify that failure isn't a bad thing. Failure is a natural thing and an opportunity to learn from your mistakes. Every successful person has failed and struggled at some point. Being successful is not easy. If it wereeasy, everybody would be successful. I know you saw so many ads about create millions without any work orany time. But that's not the reality. If you want to build something successful, you have to be patient. It isn't a fast process. Just think about a few successful people. They failed sometimes but they never gave up, that's why they achieved their goals. While some people give up when they encounter obstacles, the successful people stand up and learn from their mistakes.

Secondly, there's a lot of work to being successful. You have to put in the work. I don't care if you have a full-time job, I don't care if you have no time. Let's find a way to work as much on your online business as possible. If your goal is strong enough, I'm sure you can put in the work. You cannot be lazy.

My next advice is to have faith. You have to believe that you can do it. Read success stories. Find people who have already achieved what you want. If they can make it, you can make it too. It's not a scam, it works. If you have faith, you will take action and taking action is the key to building a successful online business.

Okay, so commit yourself and think long-term. You won't be successful and rich by tomorrow. However, if you start working on your business today, you will be thankful for it even a year later. I will show you the map, the strategies, but you must work hard and take action.

Step 2: What Is Your Passion? Finding Your Niche

A niche is a segment, a market that you need to focus on. A niche has people with the same needs and wants. Your task as an internet marketer is to satisfy their needs. If you want to fulfill them successfully, you need to inquire about this topic. That's why you need to answer the following questions. What is your passion? What is your hobby? What do you do in your free time? It must be something that you love to learn, that you're passionate about.

The three biggest niches are health, money, and relationships. These are the three biggest areas that people have problems with. However, it doesn't mean that you have to choose from them. You really need something that you're passionate about. Remember, you need to focus on the long-term, not the short-term. If you choose a topic what you don't care, that's not long-term thinking. Try to find something that you enjoy studying. The best thing would be to teach while you learn.

Every business has a niche. Offline businesses are based around a niche too. You can't sell to everybody, because every person is different and they have different difficulties and pains. You can find subniches too, which are more narrow. This allows you to help people and focus on a more concrete topic.

Okay, so if you're interestedin a topic and you choose that as a niche, you'll have an advantage. Find something that you would learn anyway. You can improve yourself and your niche too this way. However, do research before you commit yourself to a niche. Do a search on Google, YouTube or Amazon. Try to find forums and blogs, Facebook groups related to this niche. If you can find a few, it means that the niche has a market.

If you've found your niche, create your avatar. Your avatar is an imagined person in that certain niche. Write down everything about this person. What does the average day look like? What is their pain, their attitude? How old are they? What is the gender? Do they have a family? Are they married? Do they have children? If yes, how many? So write down everything. Having your avatar is very important to know because you'll have to find the right people, and your avatar will help you with that.

Some examples for niches include arts & entertainment, business/investing, computers/internet, sports, travel, cooking, education, self-help, health & fitness, parenting & families, politics, spirituality, languages, home & garden, employment & jobs, and so on.

Some examples for subniches in health & fitness include beauty, sleep& dreams, meditation, spiritual health, diets & weight loss, nutrition, remedies, exercise & fitness, and yoga. You can narrow your niche for men or just for women so that your niche can be men's health or women's health. Some examples for subniches in self-help include dating, eating disorder, marriage & relationship, time management, success, self-esteem, stress management, motivation, and public speaking.

The exercise for this chapter is to answer the questions at the beginning of this chapter and write down some of your ideas. Choose the niche that you are most interested about. After that, create your avatar, your ideal customer. Write down everything about him/her. You can even give him/her a name. You will use this avatar later when you plan your marketing.

Step 3: Build Your Brand

If you want to be successful and want to think long-term, you need a brand. A brand is a name. This name is related to your niche. You can have a website/blog or social media platforms, a podcast for your branding. Your logo is also related to your brand.

Why do you need a brand? A brand can create trust, credibility, likeability, and awareness. If you'd have a chance to choose, which product would you buy? A simple cola drink with no name behind it or Coca-Cola? You can more likely trust a product/or service with a brand behind it and you are more likely to buy that product. Or think about Apple. Apple is a brand. Moreover, Apple is all about the brand. Apple fans are loyal to the brand. Many people say "without the brand, Apple would be dead". Apple is not about computers or mobile devices, it's a passion. A brand has a value, it's very important.

The goal is to keep in touch with your customer. Don't let them forget you. You need to build trust and likeability. Create a website or blog, or you can use some of the social media platforms to keep in touch with your visitors. Creating content is not just for selling. By creating content, you can attract people to you. We live in a world where you can find content everywhere. Content is king. If you provide value, people are going to buy from you, because they know that you can help them. They know you, they trust you. Content can help you create a brand.

Your goal is not to build a business, your goal is to build a brand. Your goal is not to sell as many products as you can, your goal is to build a brand. You need to help to your customers. By building a brand, you can sell anything. Customers have feelings and emotion for brands. The most successful businesses have abrand. That's the key. That's the long-term. If you want your business to grow and become sustainable, you need a brand. The other advantage of building a brand is to other people can't complete with you.

Okay, so how can you build a brand? First of all, you need to choose a name. Don't try to be a perfectionist with that, but choose something that explains your vision. You also need to make sure that your chosen name is available.

You can easily create a website. First, you need a hosting account like Bluehost and a domain name. Bluehost is really an inexpensive option. Your domain is name is your site's URL. Bluehost can give you a free domain name. However, you can buy your own domain name for example on GoDaddy too. Then you can set up a WordPress account, which is very easy to use. WordPress is a free blogging platform, and you can use it to create your website. Most websites run on WordPress. Anyone can set this up. It's really fast and inexpensive.

Step 4: Traffic Is The Key

Traffic is the key. Why? Because without traffic you'll have almost no sales. As I mentioned before, you need to create content. But without traffic, it's all useless. So now your goal is to get traffic to your blog/website. Getting buyers is not easy, you need to build a connection, a relationship with them.

The first way is Google. Google is a search engine, and people go to Google to get info. Google has a lot of traffic and Google loves content. Having high-quality content is a positive thing in the eyes of Google. Google can identify if your content is relevant to the keywords that people search for. Many people use blogs to get Google to notice them. If you intend to start a blog centered on certain keywords, you must be careful not to spam. Instead, write a high quality blog post that will help your readers. This way, they'll spend a lot of time on it instead of quickly leaving the page. A high bounce rate may negatively affect your standing.

The second is using YouTube. YouTube is also a search engine. You can give a deeper level of value with YouTube, so it is quality traffic. Being able to rank your videos is similar to using Google to rank your site. The most important thing is to optimize your title and use keywords. Make sure to use links in your description. Also, make sure your video matches your description. If you promise people that your video will teach them something and it doesn't, you'll only end up upsetting them.

The second is using YouTube. YouTube is also a search engine. You can give adeeper level of value with YouTube, so it is quality traffic. Being able to rank your videos is similar to using Google to rank your site. The most important thingis to optimize your title and use keywords. Make sure to use links in your description.

Social media (Facebook, Instagram, Twitter, Pinterest, Google+, etc.) is an incredible asset. Again, the key is to have high-quality content. Share as much as you can. You can share personal things too. Try to engage your visitors and share your content with their friends.

Using podcasts is quite a new and powerful way because people can use a podcast while they're doing different things. A podcast is an audio file. It's not as competitive as the other options.

You can publish Kindle books on Amazon very inexpensively. You can put it up for $0.99 and you can get thousands of downloads. In your Kindle book, you can link to your website or product. The only way to communicate to your readers later is to funnel them to your website. Make sure to have high-quality content in your Kindle book and give value for your readers. Build a relationship with them and provide value.

Doing an interview with other people can also get traffic to you. A guest blog is also quite helpful. All you need to do is to post something relevant to the blog. But don't post your work. Guest blogging is a way to introduce yourself to potential customers. You must give them a reason to want to head to your own blog. If you post below average content, you will be wasting your time and wasting a huge opportunity to expand your customer base. These are just other bonus strategies.

If you already have visitors, you can communicate with them via email, and you can send them to your blog/website over and over again. Later on, I will explain in more detail how you can build an email list.

There are also paid traffic methods like Facebook ads. With Facebook, you can target. But I don't recommend this in the beginning. Try to keep your cost low in the beginning. Later if you have a lot of profit, you can spend on advertising, but until then, try to get free traffic.

These are the basic strategies, but you can learn more about getting traffic if you'd like. I advise following Digital Marketer. You can learn a lot from them about internet marketing. I just want to give you a big overview about this. In the next chapter, I will explain more advanced strategies.

To sum up, getting value isn't about selling, it's about adding value and helping people. Don't be afraid to give high-value stuff for free. It will return to you.

Step 5: How To Create An Online Business

In this chapter you will read an incredible strategy, the core thing to create a successful and profitable online business. This strategy is known as sales funnel. Maybe you heard about it before. You can use this for any kind of business.

The first step is free stuff. Giveaway something for free. It can be a blog post, a YouTube video, a podcast. Most people like videos, it's a very powerful way to start. Give your visitor a step-by-step guide or some useful tips, advice. It must be high value as you want them to buy from you. If they get very high-quality content for free, they will buy your products because they will know that it will also be high quality, because they already trust you, like you, and connect with you. So get them on your email list with this free giveaway. You'll give this free stuff in exchange for their email address.

The next step is the front end offer. After you get your visitor's email address, don't start telling them to buy things from you and don't fill their inbox with offers. Instead, you first need to survey them. What would they like? What challenges do they have? They will tell you what they want, what their challenges are. So you will know what can be your frontend offer. Don't be afraid. People would rather buy a product than search for solutions for their problems for hours. I know that all information is available for free on the internet, but people don't want to spend so much time searching for this information. This frontend offer can be an ebook, a video course, etc. You don't have to give it away for free but try to keep the price low. You can create more frontend offersthatfunnel into your core offer, which is the next step.

After that, sell the core offer. This is something that's a more advanced training program. In your frontend offer, you give some basic tips and information, but in your core offer, you have to give something of higher value—a step-by-step ultimate training program. Of course, you will know exactly what to sell because you will have taken the time to listen to the concerns of your visitors. When your visitors learn that you've made a product that will solve their issues, they will take notice. Thus, the price of this can be higher because they trust you more after your front end offer. The next part is the upsell. This is more advanced training. This will help your customer take it to the next level. This is for people who want more from you. This is something which isn't covered in the more basic products. The upsell price is higher, but it depends on the market you're in. You can use a reoccurring fee on a monthly basis.

The next piece is cross promotion. This is for further serving your customers. Cross promotion is selling other products/services that can help them. This product/service can be your own product, but you can share other people's products as well. That is called affiliate marketing, but I will tell you more about it later.

The final piece is coaching and consulting. However, this is active income, not passive. So there will be a need for your coaching but don't offer this for everyone because your time is limited. You can charge a lot more per hour for it.

A sales funnel is also useful for getting traffic, because people will find your free offer.

It all starts with a free giveaway. This will cost you money and time, but you need to offer it for free or inexpensively. Why is it good for you? Because after that you're able to promote more things. So start with the frontend, but the money is in the backend. The majority of people don't buy, they just want free stuff. That's okay, but a lot of people want more. They will buy. They are very valuable. Your task is to find your niche's problem and provide a solution to them. If someone buys from you a high-value product/service, they'll want to buy more from you. They want more. So offer them more and help them achieve more. You need to work on creating more products. Create more solutions that can help your customer so that you can build a sales funnel, a backend.

Step 6: Adding value

I know I talked a lot about adding value, but because this is the most important thing in a business, I want to talk about it even more.

Don't be afraid to put out content. Don't be a perfectionist. Even if your content isn't perfect, ask a question to yourself: is it adding value, can people benefit from it? If the answer is yes, then just put it out there, because it will help people. Make a difference and help people with your content to change their life.

Keep improving yourself to be able to add more and more value. Your goal is to have a lot of followers, to have followers who want to learn more from you. Trust me, they will come, they will find you.

Stop focusing on you, focus on other people. Don't focus on making money, focus on adding value first. If you start adding value, people will be grateful for that, and later they will give money for your courses/coaching.

I personally recommend making YouTube videos. At first, nobody will see them, but if you add value, more and more people will find you. After you have some subscribers, they will engage with you and your videos will rank better and better. So the key is to add value and create a lot of content. At the beginning try to record a video at least once a week. Don't let people forget about you.

Create a lot of videos around one keyword. Research as much as you can. Create "how to" videos for keywords that people are searching for. Optimize your content for that keyword. After a time, you don't have to use keywords when you have an audience. Make a list of your topic ideas and create as much content as you can. Remember, the more the better, and this will attract people to you. Try different things in the beginning. At the end of your videos, ask people to subscribe to your channel, or say "leave a comment below,"—this is a call to action. If they enjoyed your videos and benefited from them, they will follow you. Focus on serving, focus on creating high-quality content, so more and more people will watch your videos.

If you want to avoid failure, you need to constantly evolve, improve, and add value. So your goal is to add more value than anyone else. Don't be afraid, just be yourself. You will find people who are your customer for life because they will be so passionate about you and your brand. Your main goal is not to create customers, but fans, because this is more valuable. A one-time customer gives short-time success, but creating a fan is long-term. Think about Apple. Apple has fans. They are fans of the brand. They buy feelings, not products. That's why Apple has so many buyers who buy almost every year when Apple creates something brand new. Apple always adds value, always finds a way to achieve success, always finds a way to give incredible value.

Step 7: Marketing tips

Marketing means many things. Maybe the best definition is to attract people to you. How can you use the internet to get more customers/clients?

First, you need a website with a call to action. Make sure that this website converts visitors into customers. Your only work will be to send traffic to this website. Remember, at the first moment you don't want to sell, you want to giveaway free stuff and collect their email addresses.

Facebook ads, Facebook PPC (paid per click advertising), Facebook fan page, Google Adwords (Google advertisement option), SEO (search engine optimization), YouTube, Twitter, Instagram, LinkedIn, and Pinterest can all help you to attract people to your website. You can search for blog posts related to your topic and simply leave a comment with a link to your site. This is a powerful strategy as you use someone else's traffic and lead them to your webpage. You can use a lot of different opportunities to send traffic to your website. My advice is to use one strategy first and once you have mastered it, select another one and so on. Use marketing to build your brand.

Okay, so how do you sell once you attract people to you? First of all, you need confidence that your product is quality and it will make money. People buy from people who they know, like, and trust. You need to work on getting to know the person and building a relationship with them. Identify what their problems are to be able to serve them. Survey them, ask them what their problems are. The relationship and trust are very powerful. You need to make sure that there is a need for your product.

People buy things from emotion. There are the two motivators: pain and pleasure. Offer something to avoid pain or to give pleasure. Of course, pain is a stronger motivator. Use some kind of call to action and use a good headline. Not everybody will say yes, but that's okay. Keep trying to sell people. Ask people about their excuse. Sell something you would buy too. Don't sell worthless stuff.

Let me give you some pricing strategy. Price depends on the value that you offer. Starting small is always a good idea. The more demand, the more money you can charge. If you start small, you make more people interested, so then you can sell your product at a higher price. However, every market is different. Look around and compare your price with your competitors' price. The simple answer is the more value you give, the more money you'll make.

Marketing is all about finding a way to get your products out there. You need to promote a lot, reach as many people as you can, sell them as much as you can and improve this process as much as you can. Always try new things. Don't use the same marketing strategies. You don't want to miss out. Learn the new trends and adapt them. If something doesn't work, find another way to sell.

Also, don't neglect offline marketing and networking just because you own an online business. You can still print out your business cards, attend workshops and conferences and find people to network with. You can also still put out posters to alert potential customers to your business. At the end of the day, the people you meet face to face may end up bringing you more business especially if they tell others about you via their social media accounts.

Step 8: Examples Of Online Money Making Opportunities

Okay, now you know how to find your niche, how to build your brand, get traffic, do marketing and so on. This is the foundation. You can't make money without these things. But how can you make money after you do all this? What kind of opportunities exist? Let's take a look.

You can sell physical products through a lot of websites like Amazon or Ebay meaning you should have an inventory. This costs money; however, if you buy a large quantity, you can buy items cheaper.

Another opportunity is publishing ebooks, paperback books, and audiobooks. You can write your own book or hire someone to do it for you. You can hire freelancers or find a writing company to write you a book. Then just publish your book on any platform, like Amazon Kindle, and make money after every sale. You can even hire a graphics designer to do the cover for you too. If you'd like to publish your ebook on Amazon Kindle, you just need a KDP account which is free to use, and you will get a royalty (depending on the price of your book) after every sale you make.

The next option is advertisement. If you have a popular blog or YouTube channel, you can advertise something related to your niche for a high amount of money. You can find people who need a popular website to advertise his/her product, or you can use Google AdSense and make money from it.

Affiliate marketing is a good thing if you don't have your own product. Affiliate marketing means that you sell other people's products for a commission. Your task is to lead traffic to their sales page, and if a customer buys the product/service, you earn a commission from that. There are some amazing websites full of affiliate marketing opportunities, like Clickbank.

You can create information products and sell them as your own product. However, it requires a lot of time and effort, but the investment can be returned. If you know so much about a topic, you're free to do a digital product about it. However, you should learn a lot before doing this.

The next option is to make a software or mobile app. It can cost you a lot of money unless you're a software developer. You can put your mobile app on the Apple App Store and offer it for free or charge for every download. If you choose to give it away for free, you can make money while people use that app, for example, you can sell something inside the app.

We've already talked about it, but services can be another opportunity. For instance, you can offer coaching and consulting or be a freelancer. That's another option to make money online. If you're an expert in something and you have a lot of followers, there will be a need for your much deeper help. I would like to draw your attention, though, because these aren't passive income sources.

Except forservices, all of the above options are passive income sources. This means that you need to work hard and put your energy and money into it in thebeginning, but after that, you're able to automate it almost 100%. Coaching/consulting and freelancing require your time, so these are active income sources. However, you can work from anywhere, which means these provide a certain freedom too.

Step 9: How To Grow Your Online Business

Now I'll share with you a few tips which will allow you to grow your business. Of course, this isn't for beginners. These are more advanced tips. If you are just starting with your business, it isn't relevant to you. However, it can give you an idea of where you need to go. Remember, you need to work as hard as you can at the beginning, but later, you won't want to work your ass off any longer. You want to automate your business as much as possible. Okay, so I'll give the three most important things.

At the beginning, you have to do everything. At the beginning, you work in the business. That's okay because at first, you don't have the money to hire someone. However, you have to hire virtual assistants (VAs) later on. You'll need help. Hire people that are better than you. That's very important because later you need to work *on* your business, not *in* your business. Be a business owner, a manager, and have a team. This is the end goal. Don't waste your time on tasks that anybody else can do. Focus on tasks that you can't outsource, like creating content. At the beginning, you can hire freelancers or companies who have a team in place. You can find people on Upwork for constant tasks, or you can use Fiverr.com to outsource ad hoc tasks.

Having virtual assistants are good because you can easily train them to do things so you'll have more time. You can use that time to build more businesses. We talked about online money making opportunities already—use your time and build multiple businesses. Try to automate as many things as possible. You can even use all the discussed options to make money online. Think big and diversify your income. That's the most secure way. Don't use only one opportunity. Don't put all your eggs in one basket. I recommend buildingas many online businesses as you can around your brand.

Cross promote your existing products. If you have a publishing business and a physical business too, that's great. Make a book on a certain topic and promote one of your physical products in it. You can promote your information product too in your book. Affiliate marketing is powerful. You're free to use it in every business. You can always offer other peoples' products if they are relevant to the topic and can give value to your customer. The goal is a win-win-win situation. Win for you, your customers, and the owner of the product. Be creative and use cross promotion to make more money.

Some More Useful Online Business Tips

Before we jump into these amazing advanced tips, let me thank you and congratulate you on reading the book all the way through. I really appreciate it. Let's take a look at some more advanced tips.

We talked a lot about giving value. This is the core thing. As an entrepreneur, your task is to serve people and give as much value as you can. So don't do the bare minimum. Always offer bonuses with your products/services. This will attract more people because they'll think that they'll get higher value for the same amount of money. It creates more sales.

A lot of people think they have plenty of time. That's why they always postpone a purchase. Avoid this. Having a time limit pressures people to buy—that's exactly what you need. Use a counter on your sales page. You can say that your product won't be available after the time expires or it will be available at a higher price. Trust me, people most likely will buy if they know that your offer is a limited time offer and won't be available anymore at the same price. They think they're saving money, so they will buy before the time expires.

Be unique. Don't sell one single product/service. Make a whole package with a lot of offers in it so that it can't be compared with your competition's products.

The next tip is to narrow down your niche. If you choose a subniche, people will more likely feel that your product is exactly for them. I've already explained what subniches are, but think about a product called "sales training" and think about one called "sales training for online entrepreneurs". Which one would you choose? See? It has amazing power. Choose a narrow niche in your product names.

Another great strategy is the money back guarantee. There will be a lot of people who'll have doubts about your product. If you want to turn those visitors into customers, you'll need to offer a money back guarantee. Trust me, very few people will redeem the guarantee, but it will get a lot more buyers, so it's totally worth it. Again, be unique. If your competitor provides a 100% 30-day money back guarantee, you should offer more. Maybe you should provide a 110% money back guarantee. This will help you to get more customers. Remember, if you make high-quality content, very few people will redeem the guarantee.

Writing a sales letter requires a lot of expertise. However, there are a few basic tips you can apply. First of all, use testimonials. This will help to dispel doubts. Try to handle fears and write down how your product can help them. Ask customers what they need and provide it to them. They need to feel that your product is created exactly for them. Use text and a video format too as there will be people who want to watch the video and there will be people who just want to read through your page.

Conclusion

Thank you again for buying this book!

I hope this book was able to help give you a big overview of how can you build a successful and sustainable online business that can create financial freedom. But please remember that passive income doesn't come by itself. You need to be patient and work hard. As long as you have the desire, the motivation, you can achieve whatever you want. It doesn't matter what circumstances you're in. Don't let anything stop you. If there is somebody who can make it, you can make it too. Find a way to make passive income and use this amazing opportunity called the internet.

The next step is to take action. One little final tip I'll give you is that the best time to take action or apply things is right after you learn something. If you leave it until later, if you think "Okay, I'll apply these things, but first I'll do this, this and this" then you know what happens? Yes, you're never going to get it done. So please schedule time right now. Trust me, if you apply what you learn right now, that's what is going to get you the result, because your motivation is the highest at this moment.

You remember everything now, so you can make a lot of progress. You can take massive action right now. So start working on your online business.

If you need more motivation, just remember your goal. As long as you take consistent action, you will be making more money, and you will have a better life and more freedom because of it. I want to encourage you to take massive action, apply the things you've just learned, commit yourself and set goals now. Hopefully, you were taking notes. Review them and just set up some action steps that you can take moving forward.

Did you learn something new? I hope so. Then let's apply that and take action with that. That's really my hope for you—not to read passively, but actually apply what I shared with you because as long as you do, you'll make money and you'll become successful, and that's really what I want for you.

Are you still reading this book? Okay, now you can stop reading and start taking massive action. That's the most important thing. Really think about how you can take action based on this and work your ass off because that's the only way that you are going to get to where you want to go. It's not easy, but with hard work and commitment, which I know you have, you will get there. I'm confident that you will.

If I have to give you a final tip then I would say just take consistent action, always be learning and improving yourself. Sometimes, you're going to have to make sacrifices. It is going to be hard and challenging but as long as you have that mentality of finding a way and committing yourself to it, then you will be successful, and you will get to where you want to go.

I really want to just push you a little bit further than what you thought you could do before and just keep going down this path because it can be a very fulfilling path. The internet can provide so much opportunity, and there are so many ways to make money from it. I can promise you'll be better tomorrow than where you are today, as long as you keep taking action and you keep making progress. It's just an incredible gift that we've been given with the internet and what it can provide for us.

If you apply the things you havelearned, the sky is the limit. Anything is possible with this. It's just about applying yourself. Take action with it, scale it up, and keep doing it. As long as you do that, I have no doubt that you will be extremely successful with this. I want to really encourage you to keep going. Reward yourself for the progress. Make sure you reward yourself and celebrate that because it's going to allow you to do more. It's going to motivate you to want to do more of that. It's going to pull you.

I Need Your Help...

Finally, if you enjoyed this book, then I'd like to ask you for a favor, would you be kind enough to leave a review for this book on Amazon? It'd be greatly appreciated!

I want to reach as many people as I can with this book, and more reviews will help me accomplish that!

Check Out My Other Books

Below you'll find some of my other popular books that are popular on Amazon and Kindle as well

Alternatively, you can visit my author page on Amazon to see other work done by me.

Ketogenic Cookbook: Quick Low Calorie Ketogenic Crockpot Recipes with 7 Days Meal Plan

Freedom: How to Make Money Online and Become Financially Free by Creating Passive Income

Mediterranean Diet: Instant Pot Cookbook with Delicious Recipes

Alice the Superbug

Madison and Astrid's first magical journey

Intermittent Fasting: The Essential Beginners Guide for Women for Weight Loss

Chakra Healing: Chakra Healing and Karmic Awareness for Beginners

SEO 2017 for Growth: The Ultimate Guide to Learn Search Engine Optimization with Internet Marketing Tips

Psychology: How to Analyze People Using Human Psychological Techniques, Body Language Signals, Social Skills and Personality Types

Paleo Smoothies: Recipes to Energize and for Ultimate Health and Weight Loss

Belly Diet Smoothies: Delicious Smoothie Recipes to Flatten Your Belly, Improve Your Gut & Burn Fat

Keto Diet: Keto Diet Guide Cookbook for Beginners with Meal Plan and Simple, Delicious Recipes to Lose Weight and Look Good

Online Business from Scratch: The 9 Step Guide to Building a Profitable and Sustainable Online Business

Weight Loss: 20 Easy And Fast Diet Tips For Losing Weight - An Easy-To-Follow Weight Loss Guide

Ketogenic Cookbook: Ketogenic Cookbook for Beginners with 7 Days Meal Plan

Negative Calorie Diet: Cookbook & Guide Which Will Help You To Burn Body Fat, Lose Weight And Live Healthy

Negative Calorie Diet with Anti-Inflammatory Diet Guide

Make Money Online To Achieve Freedom

Negative Calorie Diet with Smart Fat Guide

Negative Calorie Diet & Clean Eating: Cookbook & Guide Which Will Help You To Burn Body Fat, Lose Weight And Live Healthy

Smart Fat: Cookbook with Fat Meals Which Help You to Lose Weight, Get Healthy and Improve Brain Function

Anti-Inflammatory Diet Guide: The Guide to Reduce Inflammation and Live a Healthy Life Without Pain

Essential Oils: The Young Living Book Guide of Natural Remedies for Beginners for Pets, For Dogs

Clean Eating: Cookbook and Guide to Restore Your Body's Natural Balance and Eat Healthy

Anti-Inflammatory Diet Guide: The Guide to Reduce Inflammation and Live a Healthy Life Without Pain

Dash Diet: Cookbook for Weight Loss with Action Plan and Easy Recipes

Air Fryer Cookbook: Quick, Healthy and Easy Low Carb Air Fryer Recipes

Psychology & Habits Of Highly Effective People Box Set

Leptin Resistance: Leptin Diet to Control Your Hormones, Get Permanent Weight Loss, Cure Obesity and Live Healthy

Negative Calorie Diet & Dash Diet Box Set

Negative Calorie Diet & Weight Loss Box Set

Habits of Highly Effective People: What Are the Habits of Successful People?

Slow Cooker: Cookbook with Slow Cooker Recipes

Weight Loss Cookbook: Meal Prep Cookbook for Weight Loss and Clean Eating

Weight Loss Cookbook: Mediterranean Diet for Lasting Weight Loss

Negative Calorie Diet & Dash Diet Box Set

Slow Cooker & Instant Pot Box Set

Children Books: Madison and Astrid's first magical journey & Alice the Superbug Box Set

Belly Diet: The Zero Belly Diet Step-By-Step Guide Which Helps You to Lose Your Belly and Enjoy Your Flat Belly

Weight Loss: 20 Easy and Fast Diet Tips for Losing Weight - An Easy-To-Follow Weight Loss Guide

Instant Pot: Instant Pot Pressure Cooker Cookbook with Easy and Healthy Recipes

Vegan Cookbook: Vegan Cookbook For Beginners, For Kids And For Teens For Diabetics With Pictures

Low Carb: Low Carb Diet Cookbook with Low Carb Keto Recipes for Batch Cooking

Ketogenic Cooking: Ketogenic Cooking With Your Instant Pot

Passive Income: Passive Income Tutorial with 7 Online Ideas to Generate Passive Income Streams for Beginners

Low Carb Diet: Low Carb Diet Recipes Cookbook for Beginners for Batch Cooking

Make Money from Home: How to Make Money Online and Escape the 9-5 Rat Race

Bonus: Subscribe To The Free Enhance Your Business Report!

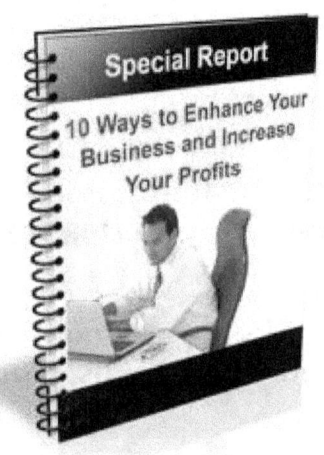

This report is going to discuss 10 important, and possible crucial facts/ideas that if implemented, will increase your business as well as your profits.

To get instant access to these incredible report go to: http://bit.ly/2tXwgKQ

www.ingramcontent.com/pod-product-compliance
Lightning Source LLC
Chambersburg PA
CBHW071219220526
45468CB00002B/670